Old COMRIE, UPPER STRATH and BALQUHIDDER

by
Bernard Byrom

The Milton, a secluded cottage, was built on the Lawers Estate in the early 1800s as the miller's house. The two buildings, apparently separate in this 1909 photograph, are actually joined together and their construction style is similar to the West Lodge of Lawers House. The cottage is situated at the lower end of a small valley known locally as Happy Valley and is adjacent to the Milton Burn which once used to power a flax mill. The two young ladies are the Misses Morrison who lived there from around 1904 until 1943. Some of the older inhabitants of Comrie remember cycling down the path past the house in the 1940s and being scolded by these two (by then) elderly maiden ladies for disturbing their hens! The inventor – name unknown although he was a nephew of the Misses Morrison – of the famous sterilising fluid 'Milton' spent so many enjoyable summer holidays at the cottage that he named his product after it.

First published in the United Kingdom, 2005,
by Stenlake Publishing Ltd.
Telephone: 01290 551122
Printed by Cordfall Ltd., Glasgow, G21 2QA

ISBN 1 84033 341 3

The publishers regret that they cannot supply
copies of any pictures featured in this book.

ACKNOWLEDGEMENTS (in alphabetical order):
Caledonian Forest Association; Anne Cameron, Comrie; John and
Joan Carmichael, Comrie; Steve Connelly and Jan Marchant,
Perthshire Archives, A.K. Bell Library, Perth; Local Studies
Department, A.K. Bell Library; Fiona MacArthur, Kingshouse
Hotel; Jenny MacGregor, Comrie; and Carol Miller, Comrie.

FURTHER READING
The books listed below were used by the author during his research. None of
them are available from Stenlake Publishing. Those interested in finding out more
are advised to contact their local bookshop or reference library.

The Statistical Account of Scotland, 1791–99
The New Statistical Account, 1845
Elizabeth Beauchamp, *The Braes O' Balquhidder*, 1993
Bernard Byrom, *The Railways of Upper Strathearn*, 2004
Ewen Cameron, *Strathyre, Balquhidder & Lochearnhead in old photographs*, 1994
Comrie W.R.I., *Comrie, our Village*, 1966
Nick Haynes, *Perth & Kinross: An Illustrated Architectural Guide*, 2000
Carol Miller & Bernard Byrom, *More Bygone Comrie*, 2002 *
James Miller, *Bygone Comrie*, 1998 *
Andrew Porteous, *Annals of St Fillans*, 1912
John Thomas, *The Callander & Oban Railway*, 1966, updated by J. Farrington, 1990
* Privately published. Available from A.K. Bell Library bookshop in Perth, S.
Campbell booksellers in Crieff, and from Comrie Library.

A stone bridge had been built across the Lednock, at the eastern approach
to Comrie, in 1799. This had replaced an earlier bridge which itself had
replaced a ford further down the river towards its confluence with the Earn.
The 1799 bridge was a substantial three-arch structure, fifteen feet wide
with angled approaches and steep gradients on either side which prevented
approaching traffic from seeing what awaited it when it reached the crown.
It was said that cyclists knew to make a spurt up one side and thank their
lucky fortune if, when they reached the crest, they were not pitched
headlong amongst the sixteen legs of the four-horse St Fillans coach! When
the railway was extended west from Comrie in 1899, the railway company
needed to have the public road diverted for a considerable distance near
Dalchonzie and, in order to sweeten relations with the County Council,
offered to rebuild the Lednock bridge at their own expense and replace it
with a modern bowstring-style bridge in a straight line continuation of
Drummond Street. This would have eliminated the angled approaches but
would have meant cutting down a line of mature lime trees that Colonel
Williamson had planted in 1884 to screen St Serf's church (which he himself
had founded) from passing traffic. A furious row ensued which lasted for
many months. The Colonel emerged victorious, the trees were saved, and
that is the reason why the main road from Crieff enters Comrie via an 'S'-
bend in the road. One of the lime trees can be seen on the right of the picture.
Beyond the bridge the buildings are Lednock Cottage, Lednock House and
the Melville Hotel (the Earnbank House Hotel since 2001).

INTRODUCTION

Comrie stands at the confluence of three rivers, the Earn, the Lednock and the Waters of Ruchill. Its name is derived from the Gaelic for 'the meeting of the waters'.

The village has two special claims to fame. One was that it was the northernmost outpost of the Roman Empire and the other is that, lying as it does on the geological Highland fault that runs from Stonehaven to Helensburgh, it has experienced more earthquakes than any other village in Britain. So many, in fact, that a purpose-built Earthquake House was established near the village in the nineteenth century to record the tremors. Fortunately for the modern village, the last significant earthquake occurred as far back as 1839.

Situated where it is, Comrie was fortunate to escape both the most serious repercussions of the Jacobite rebellions of 1715 and 1745 and also the clan warfare that bedevilled the villages further west.

In the 1700s the area was owned by James Drummond of Drummondernoch. In 1786 he let out parcels of land in feu (leasehold) for the purpose of building houses in a straight line in a new street, which he named Drummond Street after himself. These houses fronted directly onto the main street and their sasines (legal documents registering transfer of ownership) stipulate that the owners shall not 'encumber the street with peats, turfs or any such things'. In other words, they can't throw their rubbish outside their front doors onto the street!

In those days the principal occupation of the new street's occupants was handloom weaving but this cottage industry collapsed in the early nineteenth century with the establishment of power-driven mills. Victorian rebuilding of the handloom weavers' cottages in Drummond Street resulted in a mixture of shops and private houses, mostly two-storey, and nowadays the only remnants of the original buildings are the single-storey cottages numbered seven and nine in Drummond Street. These were once thatched, but were eventually slated and later given tiled roofs in the 1960s; otherwise they still present the same appearance as they did when they were originally built in 1786.

In 1800, following a disastrous marriage, the Drummond family had to sell the entire estate of Comrie to Henry Dundas for £5,950. So began the Dundas family's association with Comrie which has lasted until the present day. Henry Dundas held high office in Pitt the Younger's government and was often referred to as 'King Harry the Ninth' or 'The Uncrowned King of Scotland'. After he had retired from office and died in 1811, a prominent memorial to his achievements was erected the following year on nearby Dunmore Hill.

Before the establishment of the National Health Service there was no automatic lifeline for the poor, the sick and the incapacitated. Such people had to rely on public charity and the heritors for sustenance. Weekly church collections were held for the poor of the parish and the balance of the cost was made up by the heritors who were the local landowners. Comrie was fortunate in its heritors. The village was in an area which comprised great landed estates whose owners were, contrary to popular conception, very concerned for the welfare of the villagers on their estates. In Comrie the Dundas family, besides contributing their share of the statutory benefits for the poor, also provided them with other necessities. For instance, in 1849 Sir David Dundas gave money for coal and meal to be distributed to the poor on his Dunira Estate, while in both 1852 and 1854 Lady Dundas distributed various items of clothing for needy people in the village.

They were not alone in this. Other regular contributors included Colonel Stewart of Ardvorlich, Thomas Graham Stirling of Strowan and the Willoughby d'Eresby family, Earls of Ancaster, who lived at Drummond Castle. Even after the great estates had been sold off, their new owners carried on the benevolent tradition and both Mr G.C. Dewhurst, a Manchester textile baron who had bought the Aberuchill Estate, and Mr Gilchrist Macbeth, a Glasgow shipbuilder who owned the Dundas Estate at Dunira, carried on the tradition of distributing largess to needy folk on their estates in the early twentieth century. At the other end of the village, Colonel Williamson of Lawers spent a lifetime in improving its facilities.

Moving westwards towards St Fillans is the hill of Dundurn which, in ancient times, marked the boundary between the Kingdom of the Picts to the west and the Kingdom of the Scots to the east. After the Picts were defeated by the Scots under Kenneth MacAlpine, the whole of Strathearn became a Royal earldom.

In 1800 St Fillans, the first village west of Comrie, was originally a place of worship for the saint of the same name but, in Victorian times, it became a desirable residence for the moneyed classes of the Forth–Clyde industrial belt. Imposing villas were built as weekend cottages but, as the railway was extended there by 1901, it became possible to commute to Glasgow and Edinburgh on a daily basis. This was augmented by a stream of excursion trains and charabancs to St Fillans and these connected with the steamer sailings up the loch to Lochearnhead. By 1905 the railway had been extended along the length of Loch Earn to Lochearnhead and to Balquhidder where it made a connection with the line from Glasgow and Edinburgh to Oban.

Lochearnhead and Balquhidder are in 'outlaw country'. While most of the land had been settled by families such as the Drummonds, Stewarts and MacLarens, this was often at the expense of the MacGregors whose ancestral lands had been forfeited because of their perpetual misdeeds.

For example, not content with their run-in with the law when they killed the King's Forester, James Drummond of Drummondernoch, in 1598 and exhibited his severed head to his sister when they called at Ardvorlich Castle for refreshment on their way home, the MacGregors also perpetually supported the doomed Stuart cause in Scotland. As a result the clan was proscribed by the government of the day, which meant that it became illegal to bear the MacGregor name. The clansmen had to change their names, which they often changed to the name of their landlord or the village where they lived. Thus many of the families in the area who today bear the name of Comrie or Drummond were originally MacGregors.

The Braes of Balquhidder were Rob Roy's home ground and it was from there that he carried out his protection racket and exacted revenge on his many enemies, particularly the Duke of Montrose who had been responsible for bankrupting him many years earlier when Rob's agent had absconded with money entrusted to him. Surprisingly, after all his brushes with the law, Rob eventually received a royal pardon and died peacefully in his bed at his home near Balquhidder.

Before the time of Rob Roy, the Kirkton at Balquhidder had been an important administrative centre for the district from the time that King James III had appointed Sir William Stewart as his Royal Baille in 1480. He was overlord of 21 townships from Glen Falloch in the north to the township of Ardveich in the east and southwards down the side of Loch Lubnaig.

A little further to the south is the village of Strathyre which was once sited on the opposite side of the River Leny. It owes its existence on its present site to the coming of the military road in 1750 and the railway in 1870. Beyond it is Loch Lubnaig, which translates from the Gaelic as the 'Crooked Loch'. And that is the scope of this book.

The railway was extended from Crieff to Comrie in 1893, largely due to the efforts of Colonel Williamson of Lawers who was chairman of the Crieff & Comrie Railway Company. In 1899 a separate undertaking, the Lochearnhead, St Fillans & Comrie Railway Company, extended the line westwards, reaching St Fillans in 1901. By that time both companies had been absorbed by the Caledonian Railway which continued the line along the side of Loch Earn to join the Callander & Oban line at Balquhidder. The line was single track throughout, apart from passing loops at the stations. This picture shows Comrie Station around 1908, looking towards Crieff. The ornate footbridge was later replaced with a standard Caledonian Railway steel bridge. There were extensive goods sidings to the right of the picture, behind the station buildings, and these included a goods shed, cattle and sheep loading banks and stables for the carthorses. The line between Balquhidder and Comrie was closed to passenger traffic in 1951 and Comrie Station was closed on 4 July 1964 when the remaining train services to Crieff and Gleneagles were withdrawn.

Comrie Station, with an ex-Caledonian Railway Class 72 4-4-0 tender locomotive (British Railways No. 54500) on a Gleneagles-bound train in July 1958. The train was formed of a single coach. Although both the platforms and their buildings were still in situ, the line had been closed west of Comrie in 1951 and afterwards the only purpose of the double track through the station was to enable engines to run round their trains for their return journey to Crieff or Gleneagles. The plain steel footbridge that had replaced the earlier ornate one (see the previous photograph) can be seen in the background and beyond it is the bridge carrying the A85 main road. In 1958 diesel railbuses, then a new concept, were introduced onto the line in an effort to attract more passengers and reduce operating costs. They were not a success and the line was closed completely on 4 July 1964, one of the first casualties of the 'Beeching Cuts'. The Riverside Caravan Park now covers the site of the station and goods yard and no trace of them can be found, apart from a very short length of platform by the road bridge.

The magnificent church in the foreground is St Kessog's Free Church of Scotland. It was built in 1879 with seating for 650 and replaced the smaller Free Church of 1844 (just out of sight of the bottom right-hand corner of the picture) which then became the Public Hall. The church's building was largely financed by a legacy of £9,000, bequeathed by Miss Mary Macfarlane who was the last surviving member of the well-known local family of merchants who owned Brough & Macpherson's shop. Its style is French Gothic and the building materials were dark local stone with contrasting cream-coloured dressings and spire. The church hall is the small building in similar style to the left of it. Adjacent to it is the house of the

Church Officer or 'Beadle'. Scottish religious politics were very complex in the nineteenth century and each sect built their own churches; however, in 1900 the United Presbyterian and the Free Churches made up their differences and joined together as the United Free Church of Scotland. Subsequently, the United Free Church and the Established Church amalgamated in 1929 as the Church of Scotland. This left two Presbyterian churches in Comrie – the original church of 1805 (the 'White Church') which then became known as Comrie Old Parish Church, and St Kessog's. The former closed for worship in July 1957 and, since then, all Presbyterian congregations in the village have worshipped at St Kessog's. Following an amalgamation of local parishes it is now called the Comrie and Strowan Parish Church. In the picture Burrell Street runs in from the bottom right corner and passes between a row of houses until it makes a 90-degree turn to the right and becomes Dundas Street. It then runs in a southerly direction (from left to right across the picture) until it comes to the White Church, now the Comrie Community Centre. Its steeple can be seen in the picture above the roof of St Kessog's. At this point the road makes another 90-degree turn, this time to the left and briefly becomes Dunira Street before passing the main square and becoming Drummond Street on its way out of the village towards Crieff. The village primary school, opened in 1909, is clearly visible in the open fields behind Dundas Street.

This early twentieth-century view was taken from Dunira Street looking east down the length of Drummond Street to the Lednock Bridge which can be seen curving away in the distance. On the left, the old-established shop of Brough & Macpherson sold a wide variety of goods ranging from ironmongery, general hardware and clothing to guns and ammunition for shooting parties. Following a fire the building was redesigned by Charles Rennie Mackintosh in 1903 and is now a listed building. Melville Square is situated on the left immediately beyond the shop and the old toll house,

converted into Duncan Comrie's newsagents and stationers in 1874, is the small building on the far side. It subsequently became a branch of the Clydesdale Bank but is now the premises of Irving Geddes, solicitors and estate agents. The imposing building across the road was built in 1890 by the Commercial Bank, now the Royal Bank of Scotland. Further down the street the triple gables of McNeill's Hotel (built in 1889 and renamed the Ancaster Arms in 1898) are prominent on the skyline. Architecturally the scene is instantly recognisable today; very little has changed and the street is in a conservation area. One feature that has disappeared, however, is the cast-iron standpipe on the left-hand pavement. A piped water supply was not introduced to the houses of Comrie until around 1909; the standpipes had been removed by 1910. Similarly, the tall gas lamp in the foreground, fuelled by the Comrie Gas Light Company, is no more. Shops and businesses on the right hand side of the road were the Commercial Bank, Wm. McIntyre (draper), Archibald Gray, later Hamilton (baker with bakery behind), John Boyd (stationer), Andrew Sorley (grocer), John Stewart, Commercial Hotel, Mills Brothers (painters & decorators), Gregor McNab (cycles), Henry McKinstry (jeweller), James Stobie, later Greig (chemist), Davie Richards (grocer), Thomas Miller (shoemaker), John Muil (grocer), and the Ancaster Arms Hotel. On the left hand side were John Geddes (draper; later MacGregor's fishmonger), William Drummond (butcher), Joseph Dick (plumber), and Daniel Donaldson (painter & decorator).

The two boys are intent on their rods as they fish in the Earn, but the man on the further bank seems to have given up the fight, at least temporarily. Salmon, sea trout and brown trout can all be caught in the Earn. The photograph was taken at the spot opposite where the River Lednock flows into the north side of the Earn. Before the Lednock was first bridged in the seventeenth century, it had to be forded a little way upstream from where the man is standing. The Comrie Gas Light Company built its works on the section of land between the two rivers, just out of sight on the left of the picture. It provided gas to the village from 1854 until around 1922 when the Grampian Electric Supply Company took over the business; most of the gas company's shareholders had been local families. Its gasometers continued to be used for storage of gas until the mid 1950s but were then demolished. No trace at all remains of the buildings.

When the old Dalginross Bridge was demolished in 1904 a temporary wooden bridge was constructed across the River Earn opposite the end of Ancaster Lane. When this bridge was swept away by floods early in September that year, a rope-worked ferry had to be substituted in its place for the rest of the month. Ropes were attached to the bow and stern of the small boat and it was winched across the river from bank to bank. Even this was not without incident. On at least one occasion one of the ropes broke and the laden ferryboat was swept downstream until the remaining rope checked its flight! The marquee-like building on the far bank is the former United Presbyterian Church (known as 'Gilfillan's Church') which acquired a corrugated-iron roof after being superseded in 1867 by a new church in Dundas Street. The building is no longer there and a small housing development named Gilfillan Court now stands on its site.

Towards the end of the nineteenth century the County Council was repeatedly asked to replace the old Dalginross Bridge but they refused to erect a new one unless the local people contributed a large share of the cost. In 1904 Colonel Williamson took matters into his own hands and undertook to raise the money by obtaining subscriptions from nearby landowners and other local people. Within a relatively short time he had raised £885 towards the cost; he laid the foundation stone of the new steel bridge in August 1904 and it opened to traffic in January 1905. It was built by the firm of Sir William Arrol at a cost of £4,700 and is over 200 feet long, with a 20 feet wide roadway and five feet wide pavements on each side. Colonel Williamson took a keen interest in the progress of the new bridge and, in spite of being in his seventies, could often be seen waist-deep in the river discussing its details with the engineers. Although being of an advanced design for its time, the bridge was built to carry the traffic loads of the early 1900s and had to be strengthened in 2001. The large building beyond the bridge is the old parish church of 1805, built with seating for 1,044. It replaced an earlier church which attracted villagers with cockfighting sessions! The congregation transferred to St Kessog's in 1957 and the 'White Church' is now the village community centre.

Dalginross was a planned development on old Dalginross Muir, laid out from the 1740s in a grid pattern with two small squares, Upper and Mid Square, on the main axis. Early feuing conditions stipulated that the houses should face south. This picture, taken from the Braco road (now B827) around 1900, shows Mid Square and the road running north towards the village of Comrie proper. The narrow stone Dalginross Bridge that can be seen in the distance was replaced by the present bridge in 1905. In the background the Melville Monument overlooks the scene from the top of Dunmore Hill, while in the foreground the presence of a cast-iron standpipe near the road and a water pump in front of the cottage on the left shows that piped water to individual homes had not yet reached this part of the village by the time the photograph was taken. The cottage on the left is now named 'Rosewell' and has gained another storey. The pump in front of the cottage drew water from a well, which still exists but is now covered over. The house on the right was later demolished and rebuilt in a similar style, but the others beyond it are no longer there.

This 72 feet high Invergeldie granite obelisk was raised in memory of Henry Dundas, Viscount Melville, who became so powerful in the late eighteenth century that he was known as the 'Uncrowned King of Scotland'. It was designed by James Gillespie Graham and erected on Dunmore Hill to the north of the village. Henry Dundas was the fourth son of Robert Dundas of Arniston, Lord President of the Court of Session. He was returned to Parliament in 1774 and appointed Lord Advocate in 1775 and Secretary of State for the Home Department in 1791. Under Pitt the Younger he became Secretary at War in 1794 and First Lord of the Admiralty in 1804. He had also been Treasurer of the Admiralty between 1782 and 1800 and this led to suspicion about his financial affairs. He was impeached and charged with corruption in 1806 for allegedly misapplying public funds and had to resign all his public offices. Although he was subsequently acquitted on all counts, he never regained his former political power, although he was reinstated to the Privy Council. He died in 1811 aged 69.

Cattle meander peacefully along the A85 road through Glasdale on their way out of Comrie towards Dalchonzie. Until 1805 the present-day road westwards from Comrie did not exist. The old road left the village by what is now the Monument Road, but soon branched off to the left to pass through the 'Sheugh o' the Balloch', which separates Willie Bain's Wood from the Craig O' Ross road, and dropped down into Glasdale about 50 yards beyond the Ross Bridge, just out of sight round the bend in the road. The nearest house is called 'Alanna', followed by 'Hilcote' (with porch). The furthest house is not named. Its stonework and the pitch of its roof are different to the others so it may have been added later. The upstairs windows of the first two cottages may have been blocked up to avoid the Window Tax but this is not common in this type of property – it was more usual in larger houses. In this case it may have been done simply to avoid maintenance as the cottage faces directly into the prevailing wind. Apart from 'Hilcote' nowadays having a false upstairs window in front of the blocked-up original, the scene is little changed today.

The House of Ross was constructed in 1908 in the village of Ross, then just west of Comrie but now considered part of the town proper. It was built for Mr Douglas Maclagan by G.T. & C. Ewing and the design was in the eighteenth-century Scots vernacular style, low and rambling with a near-symmetrical main block which was pedimented at the centre. Mr Maclagan was a partner in the Edinburgh stockbroker firm of Tory, Brodie & Maclagan and used the new house as a summer residence for himself and his family. On 4 February 1914 the house was set on fire by militant suffragettes and was extensively damaged. The local fire brigade comprised a handcart equipped with a few lengths of hosepipe, one or two standpipes and a water key, and was usually manned by the water inspector (Jimmy Anderson) and the local street cleaner. This was totally inadequate to cope with the blaze and although many villagers turned out to try to rescue the Maclagan family's valuable furniture, paintings and antiques, most of these were consumed by the flames. The reason for the attack was that the Chancellor of the Exchequer, David Lloyd George, was on a visit to Glasgow to speak on the subject of women's emancipation and the suffragettes told the newspapers that they wanted to give him a 'warm welcome' to Scotland. The irony was that not only was Lloyd George himself in favour of giving women the vote but Mrs Maclagan's elder daughter, Miss Nan, was herself a suffragette, although allied to the non-violent wing of the movement. The house was subsequently rebuilt by the Ewings but passed out of the Maclagan family's possession when the two daughters, Miss Nan and Miss Hiya (Harriet), moved to the house in Dalginross named 'Earnhope' some time after their mother's death around 1943. Both sisters stayed unmarried and, after Miss Nan died in 1964, this line of a distinguished family became extinct. The property was bought by Muriel, Lady Forteviot, who opened the house and garden to the public on many occasions and raised large amounts of money for charity. The house is nowadays subdivided into a number of separate dwellings.

A 1927 view of Aberuchill Castle, near Comrie. The word 'Aberuchill' means 'confluence of the Ruchill' and it is possible that when the castle was built it was indeed situated at the junction of the Ruchill and the Earn, although these may have later changed their courses. The oldest part of Aberuchill Castle dates from the late sixteenth century when Colin, second son of Campbell of Lawers, was granted a crown charter in 1596 to build a fortalice. This was completed in 1602 and is probably the central part of the present house. It was partly obscured by the addition of a gothic wing in the early 1800s. Later additions were the porch in 1869 and the baronial additions to the north-west side in 1874. The walls in the original building are nearly four feet thick and all the windows, which are small and strong-framed, were furnished with iron stanchions. The principal entrance, which was then from the east and is now blocked up by the additions, was doubly secured by a door studded with iron nails and an iron gate. The grass plot in front of the building was formerly enclosed by a wall and served as a yard where the proprietor's cattle were kept safe at night. This protection was mainly against raids by the MacGregors who were active in the Glenartney forest. The estate came into the hands of a branch of the Drummond family in 1704 and remained in their possession until 1853 when it was bought by George L.L. Dewhurst, a cotton magnate from Manchester. Robert Burns visited the castle in the course of his Highland tour and noted in his journal that he received a cold reception there. On one of his escapades Rob Roy is said to have jumped from an upstairs window into the upper branches of a tree to avoid capture. The tree is no longer there. By 1966 the castle and estate were owned by Williams Mostyn-Owen. It survived a bad fire in 1994 and has been rebuilt. The fire occurred 80 years almost to the day after the Suffragettes tried unsuccessfully to burn it down on the same night that they set fire to the House of Ross. Aberuchill is currently owned by an American syndicate and is used as a shooting lodge.

In 1784 Viscount Melville bought the Dunira Estates from the Drummonds and built a small house which he later enlarged. In 1801 he bought the estate of Comrie lying between Dunira and the River Lednock and in 1803 began to build a new mansion house near the Boltachan Burn. The house was completed in 1809 at a cost of £11,802. In 1824 his son, the second Viscount Melville, sold most of the Dunira Estate to his kinsman, Sir Robert Dundas, Baronet of Beechwood, who built a walled garden in 1824 and added the West Lodge in 1827 – both survive today. Sir David Dundas succeeded to the estate in 1835 and in 1852 he built the mansion pictured here, half a mile east of the old house because the Boltachan Burn was liable to flooding. It was extended in 1864 and given large landscaped gardens, and a pinetum was added by 1870. In 1919 Sir George Dundas sold the entire Dunira Estate except for Comrie House and Lednock Wood to George Alexander Macbeth, a wealthy Glasgow shipbuilder, who promptly gave it as a wedding present to his son, William Gilchrist Macbeth. William made extensive alterations which gave a great deal of work to the surrounding district in the years after the First World War and also commissioned terraced gardens between 1920 and 1922. On the outbreak of the Second World War the Gilchrists moved into Home Farm and the mansion became a military convalescent hospital for the duration of the war. In December 1947, just as the family were preparing to move back into Dunira, a disastrous fire broke out and destroyed the greater part of the building. After William's death in 1948, Mrs Macbeth and her daughters stayed on at Home Farm for a further two years before the estate was sold in 1950 and fragmented into various private ownerships. The ruins of the house were subsequently demolished, apart from the east gable and an adjacent office which remain today.

A post office was first established in the village around 1849 under the charge of Miss Walker, daughter of Mr D. Walker of the Drummond Arms. The business was conducted in the cottage immediately east of the inn, now named 'Shoemakers Cottage'. Miss Walker gave up the business around 1865 and James Neish, assisted by his daughters, carried on the business in the house now named 'Ingleside'. The telegraph was introduced in 1876. Mr Neish retired in 1889 and the business was taken over by Miss Ferguson and run from a cottage at the east end of the village, next to Station Road. In 1902 Miss Ferguson married James Scott and left the village for a while, giving up the business to her sister, Miss Jessie. In 1907 she returned to St Fillans and her husband was appointed postmaster. In 1911 the cottage was rebuilt with an upper storey into the form shown in the picture. It is nowadays a private house named 'Cairndhu Cottage', but the inlet in front of the cottage, where vehicles used to pull in, is still there. A narrow lane named Drummond Lane runs between the cottage and the adjacent houses which are named 'Dunollan' and 'Earnbank' respectively.

The arrival of the parcels post was probably one of the day's highlights for the old worthies sitting at the table outside the post office. At the time when the original post office opened in 1849, a stagecoach was run by the proprietor of the Drummond Arms Hotel in Crieff between that town and Killin, calling at St Fillans for an hour's break and conveying the mails to places en route. After the coach service was withdrawn, a mail gig ran until the completion of the railway to St Fillans in 1901. The clothing of the man delivering the parcels looks like a railway uniform so he had probably brought them from the station on the hillside behind the village. Although the photograph shows Mrs Scott (nee Ferguson) handing a parcel to a customer, the railway company used to deliver parcels twice a day free of charge to tradesmen throughout the village.

The railway began extending from Comrie to St Fillans in 1899 and opened to traffic on 1 October 1901. It was built by the Lochearnhead, St Fillans & Comrie Railway Company, which ran out of money when the line had almost reached St Fillans and had to be rescued financially by the Caledonian Railway Company. The station was situated on the hillside above the village, next to Littleport Farm, and consisted of a main westbound platform, on which stood the offices, and an island platform for eastbound trains. To the right of this were quite extensive sidings as there was a considerable amount of goods traffic on the line. Work on the next section of line had begun in June 1901 but, when the contractor died only six months later, the navvies were suddenly thrown out of work and a soup kitchen had to be opened in the village until work could restart under a new contractor. The line was eventually completed through to Lochearnhead in 1904 and Balquhidder Junction in 1905 but, after a relatively short operating life, it was closed between Balquhidder and Comrie in 1951. Fortunately, these handsome station buildings have been preserved and are now the offices of a caravan park built on the site of the station and goods yard.

A placid 1920s scene on the main road out of St Fillans towards Comrie. The Drummond Arms is just out of the picture to the left. In Victorian times the demand for feus (leaseholds) increased dramatically as well-off visitors began to appreciate the scenery and healthy climate of Loch Earn. In 1872 the Caledonian Railway Company inaugurated a circular tour of the district with coaches running from Crieff to Lochearnhead and back with an hour's break at St Fillans for lunch. This inspired moneyed visitors from the industrial towns and cities to begin building spacious villas. At first these homes were occupied by retired people or used as weekend cottages, but when the railway reached St Fillans in 1901 it became possible for businessmen to commute daily from their lochside villas to their offices in Glasgow and Edinburgh. The nearest cottage is 'Shoemakers Cottage', formerly the post office of 1849. Next is 'Inverearn', then an empty space (now occupied by 'Bronwen House'), followed by 'Rosehill' and finally 'Lochiel'.

In this Edwardian picture the magnificence of the Drummond Arms Hotel contrasts starkly with the ramshackle appearance of the thatched cottage in the foreground. The scene is on the road through the village (now the A85) towards Lochearnhead. 'Shoemakers Cottage' is next to the hotel, followed by the two-gabled villa named 'Inverearn' which is set back from the road. The old thatched cottage has nowadays been replaced by 'Bronwen House', while the gate of 'Rosehill' is nearest the camera. In spite of St Fillans' reputation as a salubrious location, it is obvious from the standpipe in the foreground that piped water to individual houses had not yet been installed throughout the village. The wooden footbridge on the left of the picture crossed the River Earn from opposite the Drummond Arms Hotel to the south side where the St Fillans Highland Games have been held since 1819. They were organised by the St Fillans Highland Society, membership of which included most of the nobility and gentry of West Perthshire who used to appear at the annual gathering attired in full Highland costume.

The original clachan in the area of St Fillans existed on the hillside at the entrance to Glen Tarkin but was inconvenient and uncomfortable. Consequently the families were removed to the foot of the loch and their cottages in Glen Tarkin fell into ruin. This new eighteenth century village, which was known variously as Port of Lochearn, Meikleport or Portmore, was refounded as St Fillans in 1817 when the first feus (leaseholds) were granted by Lord Gwydyr, husband of Clementina Drummond, heiress to the Drummond Estate. At that time it consisted of a few thatched houses, a limekiln, a brewery and, of course, a distillery. The village was described at the beginning of the nineteenth century as consisting of a single row of houses, some of them two-storied and generally slated, which extended for upwards of half a mile. The rest of the feu-ground, chiefly behind and towards the west end of the village, was partly converted into gardens in front of the houses. Very few of these buildings now remain, having given way to larger and more ornate residences. The feus were let at nominal feu-duties and it was arranged that every cottage should have a few feet of ground in front of it wherein to grow flowers. A two-storey inn was also erected which, in later years, became the Drummond Arms. This was originally built by Alexander Stewart, better known as 'Alaster More'. In 1821 the St Fillans Highland Society built an additional wing in which to hold their meetings and dinners. A white marble oval tablet, bearing

their inscription, was built into the west-facing wall and it is still there. Around 1872 the inn was rebuilt by Andrew Heighton Jnr in a flamboyant Italianate style. The prominent building towards the left of the picture is the church and the area between them is occupied by Victorian villas. Near the east end of the loch is a healing well of miraculous properties, described in the first *Statistical Account* of 1792. There was a pilgrimage to the well each year on 1 May and 1 August. In 1791, for example, 70 men, women and children visited it and either walked or were carried round the well three times from east to west; they both drank the water and bathed in it. Then they threw white stones onto St Fillan's cairn and left behind some rags of linen clothing or woollen cloth as tokens of their confidence and gratitude. Anyone suffering from rheumatism of the back had to climb the nearby hill and sit on the rock on the summit which was said to form a chair for the saint. The sufferer would then lie on his back and be pulled by the legs to the bottom of the hill. The minister who wrote the 1792 *Statistical Account* commented that this treatment was reckoned to be very efficacious. If he meant that very few people ever returned for further treatment of this kind, he was probably right!

Neish Island, a former crannog (a prehistoric man-made island), was at one time the fortress of the clan of the same name from 1250 until the mid-fifteenth century. They were one of the smaller clans in the area and, after a set-to with the MacNabs at Glenboltachan in which they were defeated, they were reduced to plundering the surrounding countryside and then retreating to the security of their island fortress. They lived in this manner until 1612 when they ambushed a MacNab manservant who was returning from Crieff via Glen Lednock with provisions for the MacNab chieftain's Christmas feast. They manhandled the servant, stole the provisions and carried them off to their island fortress where they gorged themselves until they fell into a drunken stupor. The insult of losing their Christmas provisions was too much for the MacNabs to bear and their chieftain's twelve sons carried a boat overland from their base at Kinnell on Loch Tay, rowed out to Neish Island and took the fortress by surprise. The Neish clan were totally unprepared and were slaughtered to a man, the only survivor being one young boy from whom all present-day holders of the name Neish are said to be descended. The MacNab sons returned to their father in triumph, taking with them the severed head of the Neish chieftain which has, ever since, featured on the Clan MacNab crest.

Edinample Castle was built in the sixteenth century by the sinister Sir Duncan Campbell of Glenorchy, better known as Black Duncan of the Cowl, who schemed to have the local MacGregors outlawed in order to obtain their lands. It is said that the mason who built the castle was pushed off the parapets by Black Duncan himself in order to avoid payment for his work! Extended in both the eighteenth and early twentieth century, by 1939 it was owned by the Waters family whose two daughters attended St Hilda's School in Edinburgh. After the outbreak of the Second World War they arranged for the entire school to be evacuated to Edinample, but the building proved too small and unhygienic for the purpose and the school later removed itself to Ballikenrain Castle at Balfron. The castle subsequently lay unoccupied for many years and, in spite of having a number of different owners, was derelict by the late 1970s. This picture appears to show the castle at the nadir of its fortunes but, fortunately, it was subsequently purchased by its present owners who have restored it to its former glory.

These cottages stand at the side of the road from St Fillans at the approach to Lochearnhead. They have now been combined into a single house named 'Briar Cottage'. This picture shows the cottages with thatched roofs. A few years later the old thatch was replaced by, of all things, corrugated tin! The recent sympathetic (and very expensive) restoration to their original appearance gained their owner a civic award and they are now a comfortable bed & breakfast establishment. The main A85 road runs close to the loch side at this point and its widening to cope with modern traffic has meant that the cottage now stands almost on the roadway – a far cry from the peaceful scene depicted here.

As its name suggests, Glenoglehead Station was situated at the top of Glen Ogle and was the original western terminus of the Callander & Oban Railway. The railway reached here on 1 June 1870 and the station was named 'Killin', but the company ran out of money and work was not resumed until 1872. The line reached Tyndrum in August 1873, but languished there until enough money was raised to continue to Oban. It eventually reached there in June 1880. The station was three miles away from Killin village and 600 feet higher at the end of a narrow winding mountain road. A coach service operated to Killin using this road across the hill, and to Tyndrum and Oban using the present A85 via the Lix Toll. On 1 April 1886 the Killin Railway was opened between the village and a junction with the Callander & Oban line at the newly constructed Killin Junction. From that date the hillside station was renamed Glenoglehead. It kept its official passenger service until 1889 and, for a further two years, passenger trains stopped here on the guard being notified at Killin Junction or Lochearnhead (later renamed Balquhidder). From then until the end of 1916 passengers could only alight at Glenoglehead from the early morning down train on Sunday mornings when it stopped to set down mail. After 1916 it functioned only as a private halt for railway staff and as a crossing place for trains. Although the line has been closed since 1965 and the wooden building removed, the platform and the nearby surfacemen's cottages remain to this day.

The steamer *Queen of Loch Earn* approaches Lochearnhead Pier on a trip from St Fillans, *c.*1926. Edinample Castle is prominent on the south side of the loch. The *Queen* was owned by Peter Crerar of Crieff who later sold his business to Walter Alexander, the Falkirk bus company. She made two return trips a day during the five summer months and, on arrival at Lochearnhead, passengers were sometimes welcomed ashore by a piper. She was eventually laid up on the stocks at St Fillans and used as a holiday home by a man from Dundee. Loch Earn's basin was formed by being scooped out by ice during the glacial periods of the last two million years. The deepest part is located near the western end. The loch is six and a half miles long from east to west and is nearly a mile wide at its broadest point. From St Fillans, the River Earn flows eastwards out of the loch and down through Strathearn to its eventual confluence with the estuary of the River Tay below Perth.

This shows the newly opened station at Lochearnhead in 1904 and the magnificent nine-arch concrete viaduct of 40-feet span by which the line crossed the southern end of Glen Ogle. The goods shed and extensive sidings are out of sight to the left of the picture. The Lochearnhead Hotel, proudly advertising on its roof that it is under new management, stands on the main road in front of the station. It took three years to build this seven-and-a-half-mile section of line from St Fillans and a further year to build the final two miles to its junction with the Callander & Oban line at Balquhidder Junction. From St Fillans the line ran along the hillside high above Loch Earn and gave the rail traveller unparalleled views of the countryside. Unfortunately, in spite of efforts to develop the line with tourist trains such as the Six Lochs Land Cruise from Glasgow, the line never fulfilled its potential and was closed between Comrie and Balquhidder in 1951. Fortunately, Lochearnhead Station was purchased by the Hertfordshire Scouts who use it as a base for their outdoor activities. Although the tracks have been lifted, the red-brick station buildings have been maintained in excellent condition.

The main road from Callander through Lochearnhead in the 1920s. The road from Comrie and St Fillans joins it from the right. The old Lochearnhead Hotel is the large building beyond the junction. The building on the left is the village post office, owned at the time by W. Thornton, and the building next to it is still a private house. The wall in front of the post office has gone, but otherwise it is the same scene today except that the post office function has been transferred to a nearby shop.

Three Edwardian luxury touring cars outside the old Lochearnhead Hotel. The notice board standing by the corner of the hotel states that it is under entirely new management so the date was probably around 1906. The hotel was originally built in 1746 to house government troops while they built the military road through Glen Ogle. General Caulfield, who succeeded General Wade in 1740, condemned the hotel as unfit for human habitation and had it rebuilt by 1751. This new building was further extended in 1870 when the Callander & Oban Railway was constructed along the hillside behind the hotel. In the 1930s the hotel was a favourite place for the well off who used to drive up from the central belt to 'take tea'. The earliest recorded owner, in the 1850s, was Alexander McRostie who was followed by Robert Dayton between 1870 and 1890. Edwin Maisey then took over, succeeded by Elizabeth Paton in 1906. In 1916 the hotel was taken over by Mrs Maben (nee McCrae). Her daughter, Mrs Chrissie Cameron, and William Cameron, took over in 1922 and ran the hotel until Chrissie's death in 1944. Her daughter Margaret then returned from serving in the WRNS and ran the hotel until her son Ewen returned from serving in the Navy, after which he and his wife Anne ran the business. They were subsequently joined in the business by their son, Angus. After being owned by the Cameron family for 66 years, the hotel was destroyed by fire in 1982. The ruins were considered so dangerous that they were immediately demolished and dumped under the arches of the Lochearnhead Viaduct. The hotel was not rebuilt and the site is now occupied by a small housing development named Cameron Court.

The original Balquhidder Station on the Callander & Oban line was situated some 170 yards east of the station pictured here and was called Lochearnhead in spite of being some two miles away from the village of that name. It was rebuilt in 1905 to make a junction with the Lochearnhead, St Fillans & Comrie Railway which ran parallel with it from Lochearnhead, but because of the difference of around 300 yards in height between the alignment of the track levels there, a further two miles were required before the two lines could join. At the same time the station was renamed Balquhidder to avoid confusion with the station which had recently been opened at Lochearnhead by the St Fillans company. From being a wayside station, Balquhidder Junction now became a place of some importance on the railway network. It was built with a platform for Oban-bound trains and an 800-feet long, 45-feet wide island platform (pictured here) which handled southbound trains at the nearer platform side and St Fillans and Comrie trains on the further side. In addition an engine shed and engine turntable were built in the 'V' formed by the two lines and signal boxes were provided at each end of the station. Access to the island platform was by a subway from road level which was about twelve feet lower than platform level. This emerged onto the platform, covered by the elaborate wooden canopy next to the platform buildings in the centre of the picture. All this changed after the branch line to Comrie closed in 1951. There was now no requirement for a junction layout so the engine shed and both signal boxes were demolished and the station was de-staffed. The end came with the landslide in Glen Ogle in September 1965 which permanently closed the whole of the Callander & Oban line between Dunblane and Crianlarich. The station buildings were demolished and the area has since disappeared beneath the Balquhidder Braes Caravan Park; only part of the entrance subway with its glazed white bricks has survived to mark the site of a once-proud junction.

The owning family of Edenchip House were the MacGregors of Edinchip and Lanrick. The estate was purchased by John Murray MacGregor around 1778; the house was built in 1830 and the chief of the Clan Gregor lived there until relatively recently when he made his home at Newtyle, near Dundee. In 1789 Sir John MacGregor of Lanrick bought lands in Balquhidder that had belonged to the Drummond family but which had been forfeited after the 1745 rebellion and run by the Commissioners for the Forfeited Estates. Soon afterwards he bought the remaining Atholl lands in Balquhidder. Many of these lands were later sold by his grandson. Since 1980 the house has been renovated and transformed into a holiday home or hunting lodge with accommodation for up to fourteen people. It is set in extensive, mature private gardens in a raised position looking down onto Loch Earn. The MacGregor family mausoleum, built in 1830, is locked away behind wrought-iron gates at the side of the Kingshouse to Balquhidder road. There is an even earlier MacGregor burial ground near the top of the glen beyond Loch Doine, a relic of the days when the glen was populated by more than a thousand souls.

This is a postcard dated 1908. The main A84 road from Lochearnhead to Callander runs into the picture from the left and the road to Balquhidder goes off to the lower right corner. The hotel was a posting house and the carriage in the picture was probably having its horses changed. The hotel was set firmly in MacLaren land; their connection with the area dates back to the twelfth century. On the site of the hotel was the hunting lodge of King James VI, built in 1571. The present building was built in 1747 by the Commissioners for the Forfeited Estates for the convenience of drovers on their way to the great cattle trysts at Crieff and Falkirk. It was named the Kings House when a garrison was billeted there during construction of the military roads by Generals Wade and Caulfield. The hotel has been extended over the years by incorporating its outbuildings. The low building on the right is now the Rob Roy Bar and the coach house on the left has been incorporated into an enlarged restaurant. The nearest gabled building now has a window in the gable and is the gift shop, while the rustic porch has been modernised and extended across the central part. Six self-catering cottages were built in the courtyard in 1990. The road was widened and realigned in 1990 so now the hotel and junction are set back from the main road, but the old A84 signpost remains as a reminder of former days.

This timber halt was opened on the Oban line on 21 June 1871; its construction was paid for by local people. It was initially named Kingshouse Halt, but in 1931 it was renamed simply as Kingshouse. At one time the local people asked the Callander & Oban directors to lengthen the platform. The directors agreed to do this, provided that the villagers supplied the timber free. In turn, the petitioners agreed to this, provided that the railway company would carry a daily mailbag for them. The directors indignantly refused, considering this to be outright blackmail, and that was the end of the matter! Trains called there only by request. It is said that local shepherds sometimes fell asleep after a good night out in Stirling and awoke to find themselves in Oban. By custom, sympathetic railway staff would allow them a free ride back to Kingshouse on the early morning train. Train services ended in September 1965 when the section of line between Dunblane and Crianlarich was closed following a landslide in Glen Ogle. Although most of the trackbed is now designated as Cycle Route 7, the site of the platform itself has disappeared under the realigned A84 road.

This view is from Kingshouse, looking along Coshnachie Braes towards Auchtubh and Balquhidder. It is little changed today except that, in summer months, a steady stream of motor cars has replaced the horse and cart making its leisurely way up the hill. The white house on the right is Auchtubhmor House which was built in the nineteenth century and, until 1974, belonged to the chiefs of the MacGregors. The larger house in the centre is Coshnachie House and the once-abandoned white buildings in the distance are currently being renovated, although the one to the far left of the picture is now derelict. Auchtubh, which is comprised of the houses in the picture, was once a crofting community but many of these residencies are now owned by retired people or used as holiday homes.

A 1930s view of the approach to Balquhidder, looking to where the 'new' bridge crosses the Kirkton Burn with Loch Voil in the background. The house on the right is 'Keeper's Cottage'. It was formerly Stewart's Tavern, one of six alehouses in the glen and often frequented by Rob Roy. The former library, now the Library Tea Rooms, is on the left. Balquhidder village is a beautiful place in the spring. Various shades of green, broom and hawthorn are in flower, cottage gardens are gay with azaleas and rhododendrons, bluebells and stitchwort peep out from among the fresh green ferns and the cherry trees at the Kirkton are hung with snowy blossom. The pale new larches among the dark green spruce bring the hills to life and the whole valley is lit up by a shimmering Loch Voil.

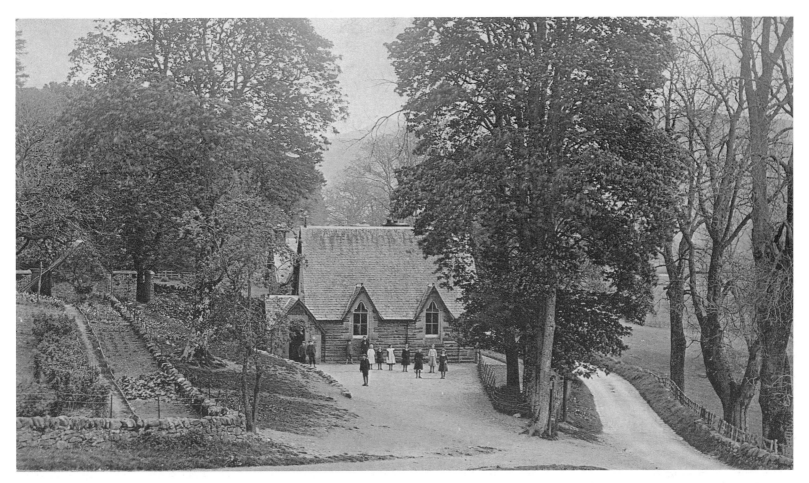

The village school and schoolmaster's cottage were opened around 1869 and were the gift of David Carnegie of Stronvar. Extensions in the 1960s comprised two new classrooms and the conversion of the single high-ceilinged room pictured here into a general-purpose room as well as the dining room becoming the kitchen. Children used to be brought down the glen to school by taxi, a hazardous task during the winter months when one false move by the driver could have precipitated the taxi and its passengers into the icy waters of Loch Voil. At lunchtime he brought the cooked dinners up from the kitchen at Strathyre school. In 1960 there were about 40 pupils and in 1962 there were 32 pupils and two teachers, Miss Stewart and Mrs Beauchamp. By 1970 the roll was down to sixteen and Mrs Beauchamp was running the school single-handed. By 1994 there were only two pupils and the school was closed. The building is now divided into two private houses. The road on the right runs to Kingshouse. The one on the left runs up to the church.

This postcard dates from around 1890. The kirk was built by David Carnegie of Stronvar in 1855 and seats around 400. It replaced the old one built in 1631 by David Murray, Lord Scone, which was itself built partly on top of a pre-Reformation church. It was visited by Queen Victoria in 1869. Two old bells are preserved in the kirk. The larger was gifted to the old kirk by the Rev. Robert Kirke, minister of Balquhidder from 1669 until 1685. He was well-versed in fairy lore and even wrote a book on the subject. He became minister of Aberfoyle and died there, aged 51. The bell was used until 1895 but now hangs by the door of the Friendship Room in the kirk. There is also an old stone, set upright, called Clach Aonghuis or Leac Aonghuis – Angus's Stone. On it is the figure of an ecclesiastic, robed and holding a chalice. Angus was patron saint of Balquhidder and on his stone, which used to be recumbent in front of the pulpit in the old kirk, marriages and baptisms were solemnised. The old stone bridge in the foreground is still standing but was superseded in late Victorian times by the present road bridge a few yards downstream.

Rob Roy MacGregor was born on 7 March 1671 at Glengyle at the head of Loch Katrine and died at Inverlochlarig, in the Braes of Balquhidder, on 28 December 1734. He was the third son of clan chief Donald Glas MacGregor and his mother was a Campbell; it was from her that he inherited his red hair, leading to his nickname, Rob Ruadh (Gaelic for red). In 1693 the MacGregor name was proscribed (banned) for their having taken part in the Jacobite uprising of 1689 and Rob became known for a time as Robert Campbell. He became captain of the local Highland Watch which had been set up to protect local landowners from having their cattle stolen by raiders and for which they paid him a fee or 'mail'. This fee was usually paid in black cattle and so it acquired the name 'blackmail' (as distinct from fees paid in silver which was known as 'whitemail'). It was only a short step from this to becoming a cattle dealer himself and he began to operate a very profitable blackmail protection racket on his own. Unfortunately, one of his agents absconded with money that had been advanced to him by the Duke of Montrose, who promptly bankrupted Rob and seized all his possessions. Having nowhere to go and no assets, Rob became a plundering outlaw pursued by the Dukes of Atholl and Montrose (the Murrays and the Grahams). They were unsuccessful in capturing him and eventually he managed to obtain a royal pardon, becoming a (reasonably) respectable citizen. He also appears to have been a well-educated man who tutored his young nephew in English, Greek and Latin. It was ironic that he met his end, not in battle, but from the effects of a wound to his arm received in a friendly duel laid on for entertainment following a negotiated settlement to a clan dispute. The wound would not heal properly and Rob died peacefully in his bed a few months later. The stone that marks his grave has Celtic tracery on it and must therefore pre-date him by many centuries. It shows a roughly engraved sword and a primitive human figure. His wife Mary lies on his right and two of his four sons are buried on his left. All the graves are nowadays surrounded by an iron railing.

In 1587 the Murray family were granted the superiority of a large part of Balquhidder by King James VI. The building on the left was built as the Library and Reading Room by David Carnegie of Stronvar in the latter half of the 1800s. Kirkton Farm is to its right, nowadays owned by The MacLaren of MacLaren whose family have connections with the area going back centuries. The old post office is on the right (see facing page) and Keeper's Cottage (formerly Stewart's Inn) is beyond it. In the distance the road winds its way to the stately Stronvar House, seen as a ghostly apparition between the trees. In the foreground a man leans on his shotgun – he may have been the gamekeeper himself, Alex Christie. Although the scene is little changed today, the functions of the buildings have changed considerably. The Reading Rooms first became the village shop and post office but are now the Library Tea Rooms, while the two buildings on the right are in private ownership.

Two customers leave the old post office at the foot of the path leading up the side of the Kirkton Burn towards the church. The building was formerly a weaver's cottage and was one of only four dwelling houses in the village in 1860. At an even earlier date there had been a lint mill at that spot. It was once the home of Duncan MacAlpine, a joiner by trade, who earned a high reputation for the fine violins he made as a hobby. On his death his widow ran the post office here. When she too died, the facility was transferred across the road to the shop that had been made out of the former Reading Room. After the Stronvar Estates were sold in 1952, the cottage was bought by Mrs McIntosh and her sister who turned the gardens into a blaze of colour.

There has been a house at Stronvar, on the south side of Loch Voil just beyond the Kirkton of Balquhidder, since at least the sixteenth century when there was a fortified house owned by Ian Dubh MacGregor who died at the battle of Glen Fruin in 1603. Little is known of the house during the seventeenth and eighteenth centuries, but it appears that the estates passed into the hands of the Stewart family. David Carnegie bought the estate of Glen Buckie in 1849 from John Lorn Stewart for £37,500 and renamed the house 'Stronvar House' after the old estate. His family had made their fortune in Sweden from brewing and sugar refining after they had been forced to flee there after supporting the Jacobites at Culloden. In 1850 he engaged the architect David Bryce to enlarge the house into an almost new mansion. These additions included the front door, entrance hall, main hall, drawing room, dining room, kitchen and the main staircase leading to five bedrooms. He also added so much land to the estate that it stretched on the south side of the glen from Invernenty (away up Loch Doine) to Stronslaney on the back road to Strathyre, and on the north side from Ledcreich down to the Smiddy at Auchtubh. David Carnegie died in 1890 aged 77 and left a fortune of nearly £500,000 in spite of all his many gifts to establishments in Scotland and Gothenburg, including houses for his estate workers. David's descendents were not cut out to be inheritors of the same mould and eventually they sold the house to the Scottish Youth Hostels Association who ran it as a very popular hostel until the early 1970s when new Fire Precaution Regulations came into effect. The SYHA decided it would be too expensive to bring the building up to the required standard and so they closed it down. Stronvar House is now back in private ownership as a high-class self-catering establishment.

This 1930s photograph shows the old meal mill that stood by the side of the Calair Burn near Ballinluig and near to the single-arched stone bridge which carries the back road to Gartnafuaran and Strathyre over the burn. The miller's house stood on the other side of the road. The mill featured in the 1960s television series *Dr Finlay's Casebook* which was set in the area and which also featured Callander as the fictitious town of 'Tannochbrae'. The little arched bridge has also appeared in television programmes. The mill closed several years ago and has now been converted into a private house.

Opposite: A street scene from around 1920. The village was originally situated on the route of an old drove road which ran on the opposite side of the River Balnaig from the present village. When the military road was built from Stirling to Fort William in 1750, the concentration of population shifted to the new road and the modern village developed with the coming of the railway in 1870. The large building in the centre of the picture is the Ben Sheann Hotel, originally the Star Inn and later rebuilt and enlarged in 1896 when it was renamed the Station Hotel. The cottage on the left is 'Clan Alpine', named after the infantry regiment raised by Sir John MacGregor Murray of MacGregor.

An 1890s scene looking down the road towards Callander, taken from in front of the station with the Ben Sheann Hotel just out of sight on the left. The memorial in the foreground is to the memory of Dugald Buchanan and was erected by public subscription in 1883. Buchanan was a famous Gaelic scholar, poet and evangelist, and was born at Ardoch Mill in 1716. He died of the plague in 1768. The memorial was maintained by the Callander & Oban Railway. The house on the left is 'Immeraich House' and next to it is 'Balvaig Cottage', later rebuilt with an inscription dated 1897. The large house after the low wall is now the 'Coire Buidhe' bed & breakfast establishment and the small house beyond it is 'Creag Mhor'. The Strathyre Inn brings up the end of the row.

Strathyre Station was built in 1870 with a single platform and siding but, as traffic increased, a second platform and siding were added. The station was destroyed by fire in 1893 and rebuilt about four years later. Because the railway company was always short of money, the only station buildings were a wooden booking office and porter's lodge, together with a small passenger shelter on the northbound platform. Under John Sutherland, its station master from 1878 to 1919, the station gained such a reputation for tidiness that in the 1890s it was awarded this ornamental fountain. This was a well-known feature on the platform for many years until the station's demise in 1965. Still mounted on its shapely pedestal carved from Ben Cruachan granite, it now graces the garden of a nearby private house. The main street can be seen in the background beyond the loading bank, the buildings being 'Coire Buidhe', 'Creag Mhor' and the Strathyre Inn, formerly the Railway Hotel. After the railway closed in 1965 the station buildings were demolished. No traces now remain of either the station or its goods yard, the area being taken up by a large car park, the village shop and by new housing called Station Court.

The early morning sun casts long shadows on Strathyre Station in April 1958. Like most other stations on the line, Strathyre was a 'passing place' and so was provided with two tracks where trains travelling in opposite directions could pass each other. The signalman has left his box and is sitting on the northbound platform holding the 'token' that will give the driver permission to continue his journey on the single-track line to Balquhidder. In return the driver will surrender the token he was given at Callander. This manner of working was standard practice on single-track railways and ensured that trains travelling in opposite directions could not be on the same stretch of single line between two stations at the same time. Unless a driver was in possession of the correct token he was not allowed to take his train out of the station. The structure on the right is for refilling the water tank in the engine's tender by means of a leather pipe which is attached to the cast-iron arm, but here the pipe appears to have come away from the arm. The other end of the leather pipe would be inserted into the engine's tender.

Camping coaches were an early version of today's self-catering holiday. They were first introduced by the London & North Eastern Railway in 1933 and proved so popular that they were being copied by other railway companies the following year. Weekly terms in the 1930s averaged around £3 per week, varying according to season. The coaches were located at many beauty spots around the countryside and usually accommodated up to six people in one two-berth and one four-berth compartment. The dining area was in the centre of the coach with the kitchen at the far end. The coaches were gradually withdrawn during the late 1960s, partly because the branch railway network shrank post-Beeching and partly because other forms of self-catering holidays had become more sophisticated.